second edition

Copymasters

Purple Level

ROSE GRIFFITHS

Heinemann Educational Publishers
Halley Court, Jordan Hill, Oxford, OX2 8EJ
a division of Harcourt Education Ltd
www.myprimary.co.uk

Heinemann is a registered trademark of Harcourt Education Ltd

© Rose Griffiths 2005

The material in this publication is copyright. The photocopiable masters may be photocopied for one-time use as instructional material in a classroom by the teacher, but they may not be copied in unlimited quantities, kept on behalf of others, passed on or sold to third parties, or stored for future use in a retrieval system. If you wish to use the material in any way other than that specified, you must apply in writing to the publisher.

First edition first published 1996

Second edition first published 2005

10 09 08 87 06 05
10 9 8 7 6 5 4 3 2 1

ISBN 0 435 02174 5

Designed and typeset by Susan Clarke
Illustrated by Mick Reid and Jeff Edwards
Cover design by Susan Clarke
Repro by Digital Imaging, Glasgow
Printed and bound in the UK by Thomson Litho

The author and publishers would like to thank teachers at the following schools for their help in trialling these materials:
Humberstone Junior School, Leicester
Knighton Fields Primary School, Leicester
St Anne's Primary School, Streetly
Orton Wistow Primary School, Peterborough
Spooner Row Primary School, Wymondham
St John's Primary School, Sevenoaks, Kent

Contents

Part 1

Sequins	Counting to 500	P1
Tens and hundreds	Addition and subtraction within 300	P2
Refreshments	Arithmetic within 300	P3
Dice sums	Addition within 200	P4, P5
School fair	Using money	P6
Tables superstars	Tables facts within 100	P7, P8
Speedy tables G/Speedy tables H	Mental recall of tables facts	P9
Fractions	Using $\frac{1}{2}$, $\frac{1}{3}$, $\frac{1}{4}$ and $\frac{1}{5}$	P10
Stickers	Multiplication and division within 300	P11, P12
More tables superstars	Tables facts within 100	P13, P14
Nine times table	Nine times table	P15, P16
Multiplying	Multiplication within 300	P17, P18
Crazy golf	Mental addition	P19, P20
Dividing	Dividing by 2 or 3 within 300	P21, P22
200 Trail	Addition and subtraction within 300	P23–P26
First to £500	Using money	P27–P30 **GP**

Part 2

Eight hundred	Counting to 800	P31
Making one hundred	Addition and subtraction to 100	P32, P33
Bags and boxes	Arithmetic within 300	P34, P35
Raffle tickets	Using and spelling numbers to 500	P36, P37
Hundred squares	Addition and subtraction within 500	P38, P39
Speedy tables I/Speedy tables J	Mental recall of tables facts	P40
Hoops	Multiples of 7 to 49	P41, P42
What's the difference?	Subtraction within 500	P43, P44
More raffle tickets	Addition and subtraction within 500	P45, P46
Multiplying	Multiplication within 500	P47, P48
Seven times table	Seven times table	P49, P50
Tenths	Using halves and tenths	P51, P52
Car boot sale	Dividing by 3 within 300	P53, P54
What's missing?	Missing numbers and operations	P55, P56
One hundred bingo	Addition and subtraction to 100	P57, P58 **GP**
Forty-nine game	Multiples of 7 to 49	P59, P60

Part 3		
One thousand	Counting to 1000	P61
Rounding	Rounding to the nearest 10 or 100	P62–P64
Rough answers	Rounding, using money	P65
Hundred squares	Addition and subtraction within 500	P66, P67
Corner cards	Place value within 1000	P68, P69
Boxes and bones	Arithmetic within 750	P70, P71
Stamps	Arithmetic within 750	P72, P73
More corner cards	Addition within 1000	P74, P75
Eight times table	Eight times table	P76, P77
Add or take away	Addition and subtraction within 750	P78, P79
Speedy tables K/Speedy tables L	Mental recall of tables facts	P80
More multiplying	Multiplication within 750	P81, P82
Halves	Halves and 50 per cent	P83
Holidays	Dividing by 2, 3, 4 or 5 within 750	P84, P85
Rough total game	Rounding, using money	P86, P87 **GP**
999 game	Place value within 100	P88, P89 **GP**
Eights game	Eight times table	P90, P91, P92 **GP**

GP Colour versions of these games are included in the *Games Pack*.

Sequins

Name _____
Date _____

There are 500 sequins here.
Colour some of them, to make a pattern.

How many sequins have you coloured?

Ask a friend to check.

Counting to 500 ◀ Purple Pupil Book Part 1 pages 8 and 9

Tens and hundreds

Name _____
Date _____

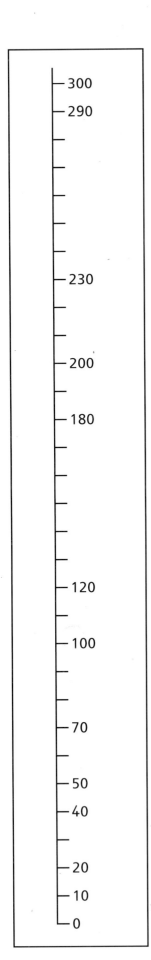

Fill in the missing numbers.

0 + 10 = 0
10 + 10 = 2
100 + 10 = 110
200 + 10 = 210

13 + 10 = 23
227 + 10 = 237
191 + 10 = ~~171~~ 201

10 + 206 = 216
10 + 99 = ~~1~~209
10 + 290 = 300

86 − 10 = 76
210 − 10 = 200
190 − 10 = 180

300 − 10 = 290
200 − 10 = ~~~~190
100 − 10 = 90

252 is 20 more than 232.

What is 20 more than:

57? 77   73? 93
92? 120   204? 224
194? 214   185? 205

What is 20 less than:

103? 83   211? 191
248? 288   115? 95

Refreshments

Name _____
Date _____

P3

How many cups for £1? __6__
How much change? __10p__

How many cups for £1? __2__
How much change? __30p__

How many sandwiches for £1? __2__
How much change? __10p__

I had 2 sandwiches and a cup of tea.
How much did it cost? __£1.25__
How much change from £5? __£2.75__

I had 3 sandwiches and a cup of squash.
How much did it cost? __£1.50__
How much change from £5? __£3.50__

Arithmetic within 300

Dice sums

Name _____
Date _____

"I made up these sums."

2 8 1 6.

```
  28      82      26      18      21
+ 16    + 61    + 81    + 62    + 86
────    ────    ────    ────    ────
  44     143      19      80     107
```

"Which sum had the biggest answer?"

```
  82
+ 61
────
 143
```

"I made up these sums."

7 2 3 5

```
  23      35      73      25      52
+ 75    + 72    + 52    + 37    + 37
────    ────    ────    ────    ────
  98     107     125      62      89

  27      23      35      32      75
+ 53    + 57    + 27    + 57    + 32
────    ────    ────    ────    ────
  80      80      62      89     107
```

"Which sum had the biggest answer?"

```
  35
+ 72
────
 107   and

  75
+ 32
────
 107
```

Addition within 200

Dice sums

Name _____

Date _____

Add these in your head.

5 9 0 = 14	4 3 4 = 11
9 9 9 = 27	7 6 8 = 21
7 2 8 = 17	1 1 9 = 11

2 0 2 4 8 1 7 5 = 29

6 6 4 3 1 7 5 8 = 40

5 7 2 8 2 4 0 1 = 29

8 6 7 3 1 9 4 5 = 44

6 9 7 7 9 2 3 4 = 47

Addition within 200 ◀ Purple Pupil Book Part 1 pages 14 and 15

School fair

Name _____

Date _____

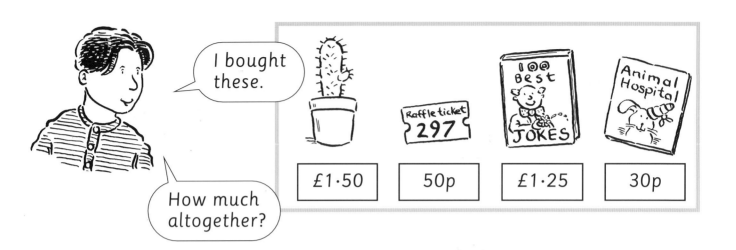

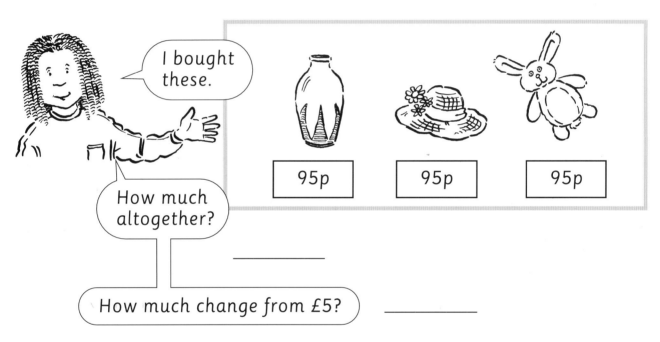

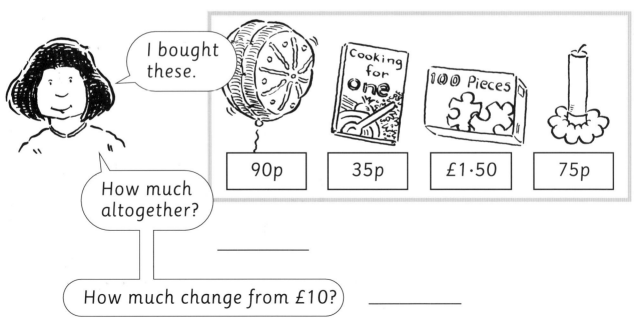

Using money

Tables superstars

Name _____
Date _____

P7

Print on card if possible.

$3 \times 9 = 27$

Use these cards to practise your tables up to 10×10.

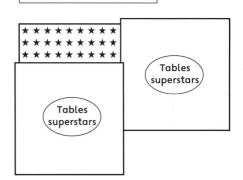

1. Colour the rows of stars in different colours (like the ones on textbook page 14).

2. Cut out the 3 cards. Write your name on the back of each card.

3. Paperclip them together to keep in your book.

Tables superstars

Tables superstars

Tables facts within 100 ◀ Purple Pupil Book Part 1 pages 18 and 19
▶ Copymaster P8

Number Connections © Rose Griffiths 2005
Harcourt Education Ltd

Tables superstars

Name _____
Date _____

3 rows of 6 stars ...

$3 \times 6 = 18$

Fill in the missing numbers.

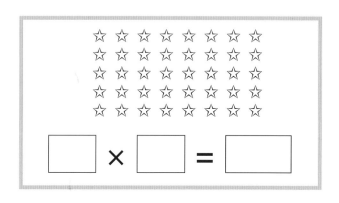

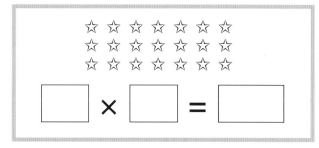

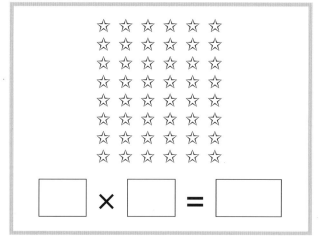

Speedy tables G
1 2 3 minute test

Name _____

Date _____

P9

3 × 5 = ___	24 ÷ 8 = ___	0 × 4 = ___
6 × 7 = ___	21 ÷ 3 = ___	24 ÷ 4 = ___
4 × 8 = ___	40 ÷ 5 = ___	5 × 6 = ___
10 × 10 = ___	18 ÷ 6 = ___	28 ÷ 7 = ___
9 × 4 = ___	48 ÷ 8 = ___	6 × 9 = ___
7 × 5 = ___	16 ÷ 2 = ___	45 ÷ 9 = ___
3 × 9 = ___	25 ÷ 5 = ___	Score: ___

Mental recall of tables facts   ◀ Purple Pupil Book Part 1 pages 20 and 21 onwards   Number Connections © Rose Griffiths 2005 Harcourt Education Ltd

Speedy tables H
1 2 3 minute test

Name _____

Date _____

2 × 9 = ___	20 ÷ 4 = ___	4 × 9 = ___
6 × 0 = ___	12 ÷ 3 = ___	24 ÷ 3 = ___
5 × 7 = ___	36 ÷ 6 = ___	6 × 8 = ___
7 × 3 = ___	45 ÷ 5 = ___	15 ÷ 5 = ___
8 × 4 = ___	27 ÷ 9 = ___	7 × 6 = ___
4 × 4 = ___	24 ÷ 6 = ___	54 ÷ 9 = ___
8 × 5 = ___	28 ÷ 4 = ___	Score: ___

Mental recall of tables facts   ◀ Purple Pupil Book Part 1 pages 20 and 21 onwards   Number Connections © Rose Griffiths 2005 Harcourt Education Ltd

Fractions

Name _____
Date _____

P10

Draw lines to cut up these cakes.

halves   thirds   quarters   fifths

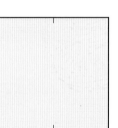 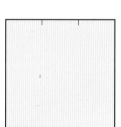 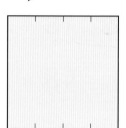 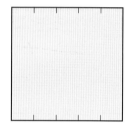

Which is bigger, $\frac{1}{5}$ or $\frac{1}{2}$? _____

Which is bigger, $\frac{2}{5}$ or $\frac{3}{4}$? _____

Which is bigger, $\frac{3}{5}$ or $\frac{3}{4}$? _____

Which is bigger, $\frac{3}{5}$ or $\frac{1}{2}$? _____

Which is bigger, $\frac{2}{5}$ or $\frac{2}{3}$? _____

I was hungry!   Fill in the missing fractions.

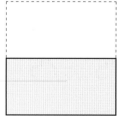 $\frac{1}{2}$ eaten

$\frac{1}{2}$ left

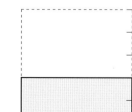 ( ) eaten

( ) left

Using $\frac{1}{2}$s, $\frac{1}{3}$s, $\frac{1}{4}$s and $\frac{1}{5}$s   ◀ Purple Pupil Book Part 1 pages 22 and 23

Stickers

Name _____
Date _____

"5 pets on a sheet of stickers."

How many pets on:

5 sheets? _____   8 sheets? _____

9 sheets? _____   6 sheets? _____

How many sheets for:

15 pets? _____   35 pets? _____

50 pets? _____   20 pets? _____

---

13 × 5   21 × 5   36 × 5   47 × 5

5)55   5)60   5)75

Multiplication and division within 300

Stickers

Name _____
Date _____

P12

4 fish on a sheet of stickers.

How many fish on:

3 sheets? _____   7 sheets? _____

5 sheets? _____   9 sheets? _____

How many sheets for:

8 fish? _____   24 fish? _____

32 fish? _____   16 fish? _____

40 fish? _____   48 fish? _____

```
  22        17        65        50
×  4      ×  4      ×  4      ×  4
────      ────      ────      ────
  88        52       ____      ____
```

$4\overline{)80}$ $4\overline{)84}$ $4\overline{)88}$

Multiplication and division within 300

More tables superstars

Name _____
Date _____

 How many 7s make 21? 3

7)21 → 3

4)24

6)36

5)5

6)12

9)54

9)36

5)30

Tables facts within 100

More tables superstars

Name _____
Date _____

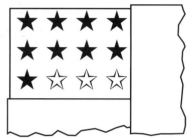

$$4\overline{)9}\ \ ^{2r.1}$$

$$2\overline{)14} \quad\quad 2\overline{)15} \quad\quad 2\overline{)16}$$

$$3\overline{)15} \quad\quad 3\overline{)16} \quad\quad 3\overline{)17}$$

$$4\overline{)20} \quad\quad 4\overline{)22} \quad\quad 4\overline{)23}$$

$$5\overline{)25} \quad\quad 5\overline{)27} \quad\quad 5\overline{)29}$$

$$3\overline{)28} \quad\quad 5\overline{)40} \quad\quad 4\overline{)25}$$

$$5\overline{)45} \quad\quad 2\overline{)19} \quad\quad 3\overline{)30}$$

$$10\overline{)80} \quad\quad 10\overline{)86} \quad\quad 5\overline{)33}$$

Tables facts within 100

Nine times table

Name _____

Date _____

P15

Cut out the eleven tables facts.
Fold along the dotted line and glue flat.

Ask your teacher how to practise with these.

		5×9	45
0×9	0	6×9	54
1×9	9	7×9	63
2×9	<u>18</u>	8×9	72
3×9	27	9×9	<u>81</u>
4×9	36	10×9	90

Nine times table ◀ Purple Pupil Book Part 1 pages 28 and 29
▶ Copymaster P16

Number Connections © Rose Griffiths 2005
Harcourt Education Ltd

Nine times table

Name _____
Date _____

P16

Fill in the missing numbers.

(10 take away 1)	9
(20 take away 2)	___
(30 take away 3)	___
(40 take away 4)	___
(50 take away 5)	___
(60 take away 6)	___
(70 take away 7)	___
(80 take away 8)	___
(90 take away 9)	___
(100 take away 10)	___

(1 nine)	9
(2 nines)	___
(3 nines)	___
(4 nines)	___
(5 nines)	___
(6 nines)	___
(7 nines)	___
(8 nines)	___
(9 nines)	___
(10 nines)	___

$3 \times 9 = \square$

$27 \div 3 = \square$

$\square \times 9 = 45$

$45 \div 9 = \square$

$9 \times 8 = \square$

$72 \div 9 = \square$

$6 \times 9 = \square$

$54 \div 6 = \square$

Multiplying

Name _____
Date _____

P17

Use tens and ones. Draw them. Then multiply on paper.

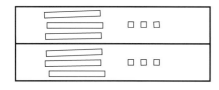 33 times 3   33 times 4

```
   33          33          33
 ×  2        ×  3        ×  4
 ____        ____        ____

 ____        ____        ____
```

Use tens and ones. <u>Then</u> multiply on paper.

```
   57          90          42          63
 ×  2        ×  3        ×  5        ×  4
 ____        ____        ____        ____


 ____        ____        ____        ____


   38          54          94
 ×  3        ×  5        ×  2
 ____        ____        ____


 ____        ____        ____
```

 ✓ or ✗

Multiplication within 300

Multiplying

Name _____
Date _____

P18

Use tens and ones. Draw them. Then multiply on paper.

46 times 2   46 times 3   46 times 4

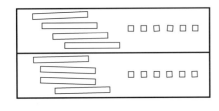 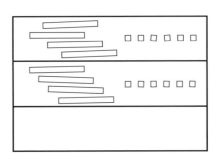 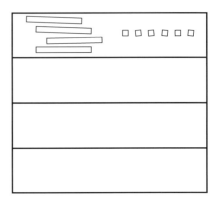

```
   46          46          46
 ×  2        ×  3        ×  4
 ____        ____        ____

 ____        ____        ____
```

Multiply on paper. <u>Then</u> use tens and ones.

```
   91        79        53        60
 ×  3      ×  2      ×  4      ×  5
 ____      ____      ____      ____

 ____      ____      ____      ____


   66        73        86
 ×  2      ×  4      ×  3
 ____      ____      ____

 ____      ____      ____
```

✓ or ✗

Multiplication within 300 ◀ Purple Pupil Book Part 1 pages 30 and 31

Crazy golf

Name _____

Date _____

P19

"What are our totals?"

CRAZY GOLF
Name: Emma

HOLE	STROKES	HOLE	STROKES
1	4	7	4
2	4	8	4
3	2	9	6
4	6	10	3
5	4	11	5
6	5	12	5
		TOTAL	

CRAZY GOLF
Name: Shaun

HOLE	STROKES	HOLE	STROKES
1	2	7	5
2	2	8	3
3	5	9	2
4	11	10	3
5	3	11	4
6	2	12	8
		TOTAL	

CRAZY GOLF
Name: Andy

HOLE	STROKES	HOLE	STROKES
1	3	7	12
2	5	8	3
3	2	9	4
4	1	10	2
5	2	11	4
6	8	12	4
		TOTAL	

CRAZY GOLF
Name: Kelly

HOLE	STROKES	HOLE	STROKES
1	3	7	7
2	5	8	4
3	4	9	3
4	3	10	7
5	5	11	2
6	3	12	8
		TOTAL	

CRAZY GOLF
Name: Asha

HOLE	STROKES	HOLE	STROKES
1	3	7	2
2	4	8	4
3	3	9	2
4	3	10	3
5	4	11	4
6	2	12	4
		TOTAL	

CRAZY GOLF
Name: Frank

HOLE	STROKES	HOLE	STROKES
1	2	7	4
2	5	8	2
3	4	9	3
4	2	10	3
5	6	11	3
6	1	12	5
		TOTAL	

CRAZY GOLF
Name: Sophie

HOLE	STROKES	HOLE	STROKES
1	3	7	8
2	2	8	2
3	4	9	3
4	3	10	3
5	3	11	4
6	3	12	2
		TOTAL	

"Who was the winner?"

_____

Mental addition ◀ Purple Pupil Book Part 1 pages 32 and 33 ▶ Copymaster P20

Crazy golf

Name ______________________

Date ______________________

Make up these score cards for a friend to add up.
When they finish ✓ or ✗.

What are
the totals?

CRAZY GOLF

Name:

HOLE	STROKES	HOLE	STROKES
1		7	
2		8	
3		9	
4		10	
5		11	
6		12	
		TOTAL	

CRAZY GOLF

Name:

HOLE	STROKES	HOLE	STROKES
1		7	
2		8	
3		9	
4		10	
5		11	
6		12	
		TOTAL	

CRAZY GOLF

Name:

HOLE	STROKES	HOLE	STROKES
1		7	
2		8	
3		9	
4		10	
5		11	
6		12	
		TOTAL	

CRAZY GOLF

Name:

HOLE	STROKES	HOLE	STROKES
1		7	
2		8	
3		9	
4		10	
5		11	
6		12	
		TOTAL	

CRAZY GOLF

Name:

HOLE	STROKES	HOLE	STROKES
1		7	
2		8	
3		9	
4		10	
5		11	
6		12	
		TOTAL	

CRAZY GOLF

Name:

HOLE	STROKES	HOLE	STROKES
1		7	
2		8	
3		9	
4		10	
5		11	
6		12	
		TOTAL	

CRAZY GOLF

Name:

HOLE	STROKES	HOLE	STROKES
1		7	
2		8	
3		9	
4		10	
5		11	
6		12	
		TOTAL	

Who was
the winner?

____

◀ Purple Pupil Book Part 1 pages 32 and 33

Dividing

Name _____
Date _____

Use hundreds, tens and ones to divide by 2.

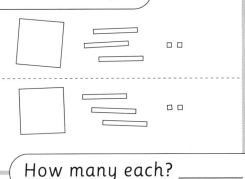

264 divided by 2

How many each? _____

$264 \div 2 =$ _____

$2 \overline{)264}$

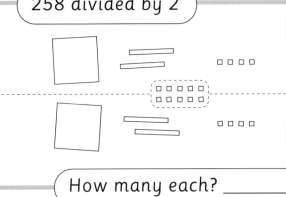

258 divided by 2

How many each? _____

$258 \div 2 =$ _____

$2 \overline{)258}$

Divide on paper. Check with hundreds, tens and ones.

$2 \overline{)160}$ $2 \overline{)94}$ $2 \overline{)200}$

$2 \overline{)236}$ $2 \overline{)190}$ $2 \overline{)254}$

$2 \overline{)152}$ $2 \overline{)298}$ $2 \overline{)300}$

Dividing by 2 or 3 within 300

Dividing

Name _____
Date _____

Use hundreds, tens and ones to divide by 3.

186 divided by 3

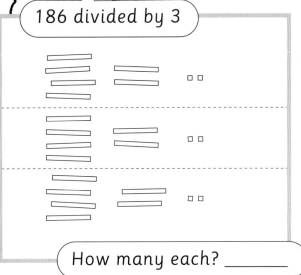

How many each? _____

$186 \div 3 =$ _____

3) 186

300 divided by 3

$300 \div 3 =$ _____

3) 300

How many each? _____

Choose how to do these.

3) 195   3) 273   3) 78

3) 111   3) 252   3) 144

Dividing by 2 or 3 within 300

200 Trail

sheet 1 of 4

Print on card if possible. Reusable.
Colour and cut out the instructions card, 2 sets of ten cards and game board.
Store in a clear zip-top wallet or in an envelope.
Include 3 different coloured centimetre cubes (as counters) if possible.

- **Before you start**

  Choose either the adding cards or the taking away cards.
  Shuffle them. Put them in a pile, face down.

     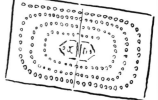

  You need a centimetre cube each, as your counter.
  Put it on the 200 Trail board.

- **How to play**

  Turn over a card.
  Move that many places.
  Put the card at the bottom of the pile.

  Your friend checks your go.
  Then it is your friend's turn.

- Shuffle the pile of cards every ten turns, if you want to.
  Keep going until you get to the end of the trail.

◀ Purple Pupil Book Part 1; **Addition and subtraction within 300**

Number Connections © Rose Griffiths 2005
Harcourt Education Ltd

200 Trail

sheet 2 of 4

Print on card if possible. Reusable.

200 Trail Adding Game **Add one**	200 Trail Adding Game **Add two**
200 Trail Adding Game **Add three**	200 Trail Adding Game **Add four**
200 Trail Adding Game **Add ten**	200 Trail Adding Game **Add ten**
200 Trail Adding Game **Add twenty**	200 Trail Adding Game **Add twenty**
200 Trail Adding Game **Add thirty**	200 Trail Adding Game **Add thirty**

200 Trail Taking away Game **Take away 1**	200 Trail Taking away Game **Take away 2**
200 Trail Taking away Game **Take away 3**	200 Trail Taking away Game **Take away 4**
200 Trail Taking away Game **Take away 10**	200 Trail Taking away Game **Take away 10**
200 Trail Taking away Game **Take away 20**	200 Trail Taking away Game **Take away 20**
200 Trail Taking away Game **Take away 30**	200 Trail Taking away Game **Take away 30**

◀ Purple Pupil Book Part 1; use from pages 10 and 11 onwards

200 Trail
sheet 3 of 4

Print on card if possible. Reusable.
Colour in and cover with clear plastic if wished, then cut out both pieces of the board (see Copymaster P26). Join together with sticky tape.

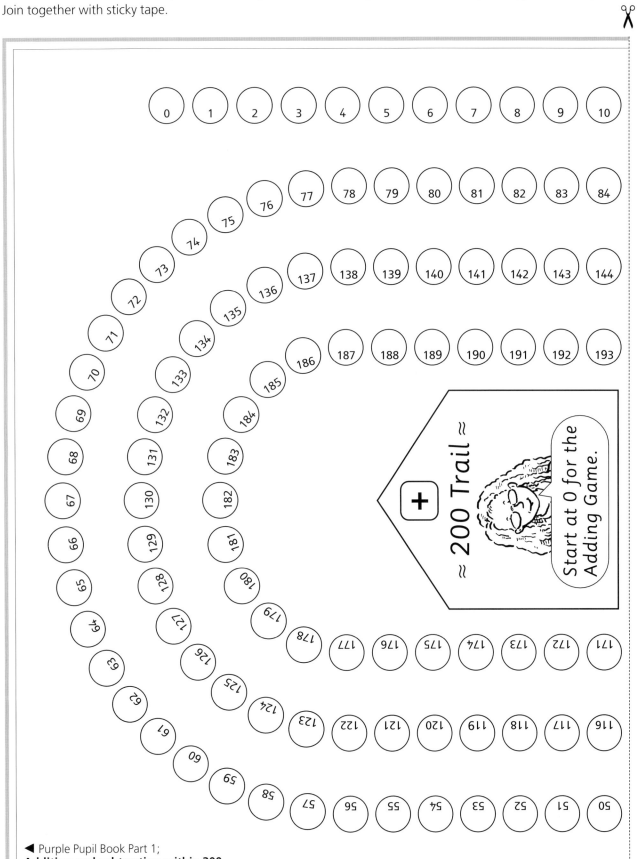

◀ Purple Pupil Book Part 1;
Addition and subtraction within 300

◀ Purple Pupil Book Part 1; use from pages 10 and 11 onwards

Number Connections © Rose Griffiths 2005
Harcourt Education Ltd

200 Trail
sheet 4 of 4

Print on card if possible. Reusable.
Join to the other piece of game board (on Copymaster P25).

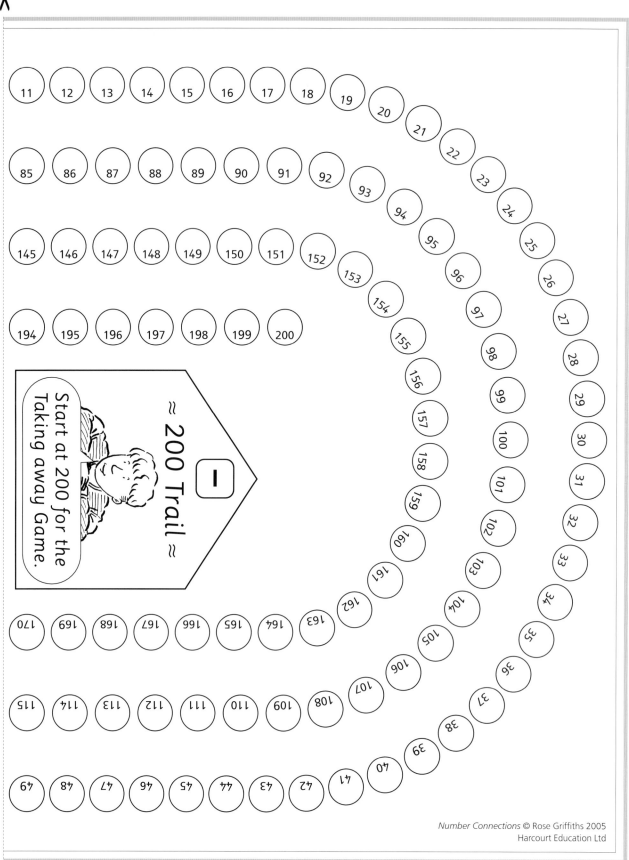

First to £500
sheet 1 of 4

Print on card if possible. Reusable.
Colour in and cut out with clear plastic, if wished, then cut out both pieces of the board (see Copymaster P28). Join together with sticky tape.

≈First to £500≈

A game for 1, 2 or 3 people.

- **Before you start**
  You need a dice, a counter each,
  up to 15 one hundred pound notes,
  30 ten pound notes, and
  30 one pound coins.

  Put your counter on the arrow.

◀ Purple Pupil Book Part 1;
Using money

First to £500

sheet 2 of 4

Print on card if possible. Reusable.
Store in a clear zip-top wallet or in an envelope. If possible, include a dice, 3 counters, 30 plastic or card £1 coins, 30 token £10 notes, and 15 token £100 notes (see Copymasters P29 and P30).

First to £500
sheet 3 of 4

Print 2 copies on apricot paper if possible. Reusable.

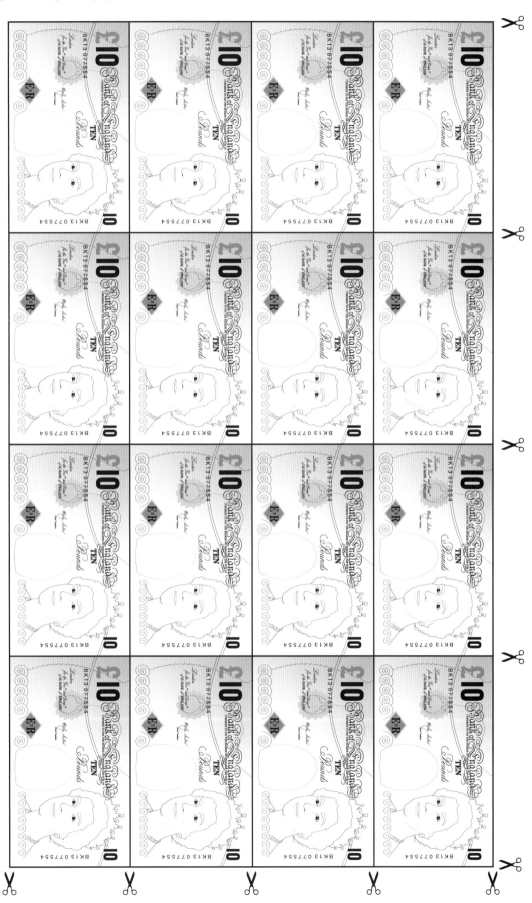

◀ Purple Pupil Book Part 1; use from pages 16 and 17 onwards

First to £500

sheet 4 of 4

Print 2 copies on coloured paper (not apricot), if possible. Reusable.

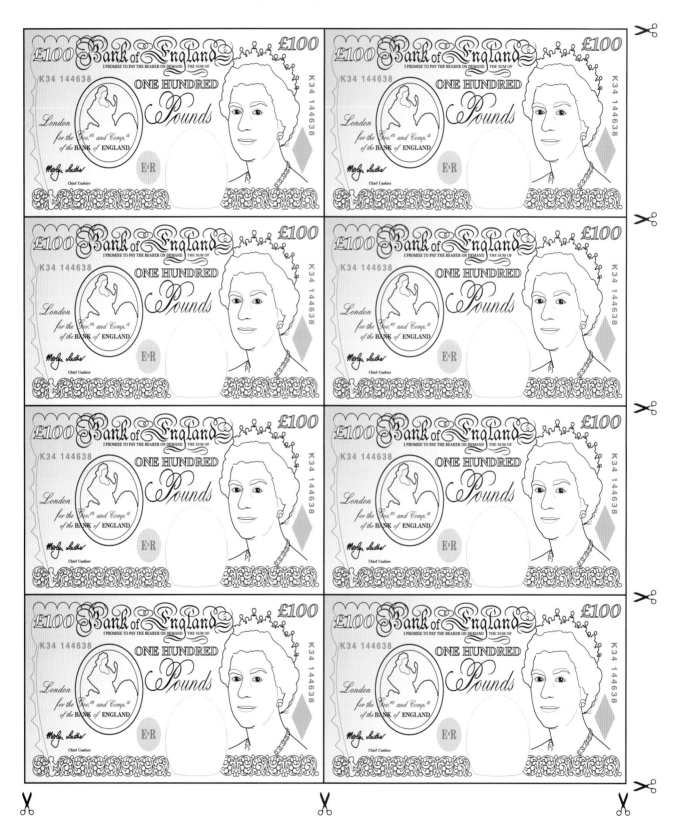

◀ Purple Pupil Book Part 1; use from pages 16 and 17 onwards

Eight hundred

Name _____

Date _____

P31

How many in each box?

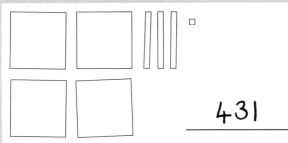

431

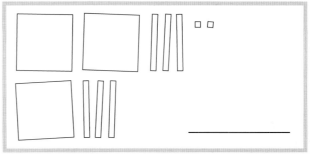

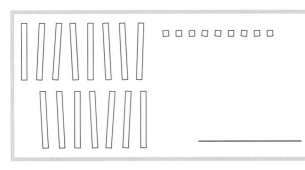

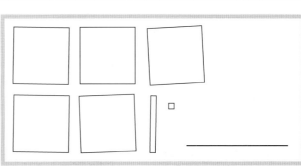

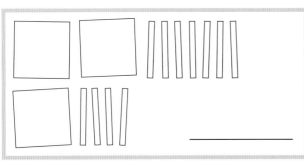

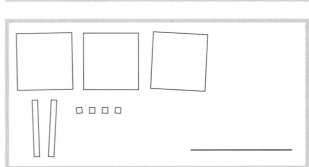

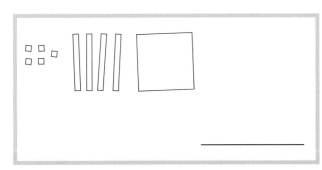

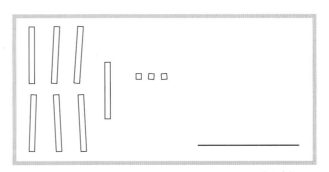

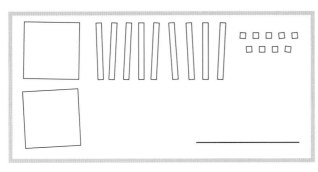

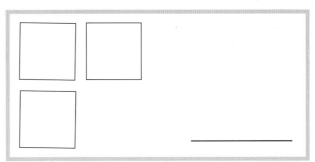

Making one hundred

Name _____

Date _____

I've got 48. How many more to make 100?

48 + [52] = 100

Make each number with tens and ones. Draw them.	Fill in the missing numbers.
(76)	76 + ☐ = 100 100 − 76 = ☐
(38)	38 + ☐ = 100 100 − 38 = ☐
(53)	53 + ☐ = 100 100 − 53 = ☐
(81)	81 + ☐ = 100 100 − 81 = ☐
(67)	67 + ☐ = 100 100 − 67 = ☐
(19)	19 + ☐ = 100 100 − 19 = ☐

Addition and subtraction to 100 ◀ Purple Pupil Book Part 2 pages 40 and 41 ▶ Copymaster P33

Making one hundred

Check my sums. ✓ or ✗

```
  45       92       36      100       89
+ 55     + 18     + 64     +  0     + 11
-----    -----    -----    -----    -----
 100      100      100      100      100


  14       28       55       73       46
+ 84     + 82     + 35     + 27     + 55
-----    -----    -----    -----    -----
 100      100      100      100      100
```

Complete.

100 − 70 = ____   100 − 74 = ____

100 − 80 = ____   100 − 83 = ____

100 − 30 = ____   100 − 31 = ____

100 − 20 = ____   100 − 25 = ____

100 − 40 = ____   100 − 47 = ____

100 − 50 = ____   100 − 59 = ____

100 − 90 = ____   100 − 92 = ____

100 − 60 = ____   100 − 66 = ____

100 − 10 = ____   100 − 18 = ____

100 − 0 = ____   100 − 2 = ____

Addition and subtraction to 100   ◀ Purple Pupil Book Part 2 pages 40 and 41

Bags and boxes

Name _____
Date _____

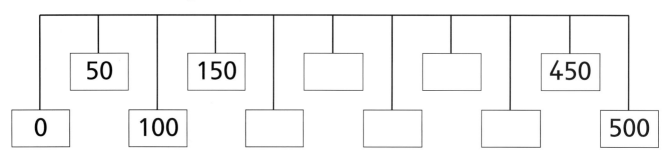

Fill in the missing numbers.

50	150			450
0	100			500

100 + 25 = ____
175 + 25 = ____
225 + 25 = ____
350 + 25 = ____
400 + 25 = ____
475 + 25 = ____

350 − 25 = ____
300 − 25 = ____
200 − 25 = ____

250 + 50 = ____
250 + 150 = ____
300 + 50 = ____
350 + 100 = ____
350 + 150 = ____
400 + 50 = ____

500 − 50 = ____
500 − 150 = ____
500 − 250 = ____

```
   50
 ×  4
 ____
```

```
   50
 ×  7
 ____
```

```
  150
 ×  2
 ____
```

Arithmetic within 500

Bags and boxes

Name _____
Date _____

P35

Look at this bank bag.

How many make £20?
_____

The CO-OPERATIVE BANK

NO MIXED COIN PLEASE

£20 IN POUND COIN

£10 SILVER IN 50p or 20p

£5 SILVER IN 10p or 5p

£1 BRONZE IN 2p or 1p

RE-USABLE BAG, PLEASE RETURN

How many make £10?
_____

How many make £10?
_____

How many make £5?
_____

How many make £5?
_____

How many make £1?
_____

How many make £1?
_____

Arithmetic within 500 ◀ Purple Pupil Book Part 2 pages 42 and 43

Raffle tickets

Name _____
Date _____

P36

Cut out these tickets.
Use them with Copymaster P37.

72	85	98	109

23	37	46	51	64

15	16	17	18	19

10	11	12	13	14

Using and spelling numbers to 500 ◀ Purple Pupil Book Part 2 pages 44 and 45
▶ Copymaster P37

Number Connections © Rose Griffiths 2005
Harcourt Education Ltd

Raffle tickets

Name _____

Date _____

Work with a friend to practise your spelling.

Cut out the tickets on Copymaster P36.

Fold the tickets and put them in a tub or bag.

Take turns to pick a number to spell.

Check your spellings here.

1	one	11	eleven	30	thirty
2	two	12	twelve	40	forty
3	three	13	thirteen	50	fifty
4	four	14	fourteen	60	sixty
5	five	15	fifteen	70	seventy
6	six	16	sixteen	80	eighty
7	seven	17	seventeen	90	ninety
8	eight	18	eighteen	100	hundred
9	nine	19	nineteen		
10	ten	20	twenty		

Which numbers do <u>you</u> think are the hardest to spell?

_____ _____

_____ _____

Using and spelling numbers to 500

Hundred squares

Name _____

Date _____

P38

Fill in the missing numbers.

351	352	353	354	355		357	358	359	360
361			364	365	366	367			370
371	372	373		375	376			379	
381			384	385	386	387	388	389	
	392	393	394				398	399	400
	402	403		405		407	408		
411	412	413	414		416	417		419	420
	422			425	426		428		430
431		433		435		437		439	
	442	443	444		446				

Use the hundred square.

395 + 40 = _____   398 + 37 = _____

439 − 62 = _____   351 + 93 = _____

371 + 58 = _____   426 − 71 = _____

417 − 40 = _____   404 + 43 = _____

Hundred squares

Name _____

Date _____

One number is <u>wrong</u> on this hundred square.

Find it and put it right.

401	402	403	404	405	406	407	408	409	410
411	412	413	414	415	416	417	418	419	420
421	422	423	424	425	426	427	428	429	430
431	432	433	434	435	436	437	438	439	440
441	442	443	444	445	446	447	448	449	450
451	452	453	454	455	456	457	458	459	460
461	462	463	464	465	466	467	468	469	470
471	472	473	474	475	476	477	478	478	480
481	482	483	484	485	486	487	488	489	490
491	492	493	494	495	496	497	498	499	500

Fill in the missing numbers.

443 + ☐ = 473

☐ + 60 = 487

480 − 19 = ☐

446 + ☐ = 500

462 − 45 = ☐

488 − ☐ = 428

405 + 27 = ☐

☐ + 20 = 444

493 − 51 = ☐

☐ + 34 = 459

Addition and subtraction within 500

Speedy tables I
1 2 3 minute test

Name _____
Date _____

4 × 6 = ___	27 ÷ 3 = ___	8 × 9 = ___
5 × 3 = ___	9 ÷ 9 = ___	16 ÷ 4 = ___
2 × 7 = ___	40 ÷ 5 = ___	0 × 8 = ___
9 × 9 = ___	21 ÷ 7 = ___	42 ÷ 6 = ___
8 × 6 = ___	63 ÷ 9 = ___	10 × 4 = ___
5 × 5 = ___	48 ÷ 6 = ___	54 ÷ 6 = ___
7 × 4 = ___	70 ÷ 10 = ___	Score: ___

Mental recall of tables facts ◀ Purple Pupil Book Part 2 pages 48 and 49 onwards

---

Speedy tables J
1 2 3 minute test

Name _____
Date _____

4 × 9 = ___	24 ÷ 6 = ___	3 × 7 = ___
4 × 7 = ___	35 ÷ 5 = ___	18 ÷ 2 = ___
6 × 6 = ___	60 ÷ 10 = ___	7 × 6 = ___
9 × 8 = ___	32 ÷ 4 = ___	24 ÷ 3 = ___
3 × 0 = ___	5 ÷ 5 = ___	9 × 6 = ___
9 × 7 = ___	42 ÷ 6 = ___	81 ÷ 9 = ___
5 × 8 = ___	45 ÷ 9 = ___	Score: ___

Mental recall of tables facts ◀ Purple Pupil Book Part 2 pages 48 and 49 onwards

Hoops

Name _____
Date _____

Fill in the missing numbers.

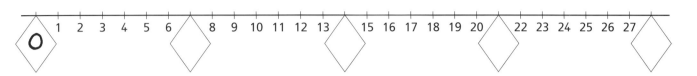

1	2	3	4	5	6	7
8	9	10	11	12	13	
15	16	17	18	19	20	
22	23	24	25	26	27	
29	30	31	32	33	34	
36	37	38	39	40	41	
43	44	45	46	47	48	

```
   7         14
+  7      +   7
____      ____


  21         28
+  7      +   7
____      ____
```

```
 35        42        35        49        42
+ 7       + 7       -14       -14       -14
____      ____      ____      ____      ____
```

```
 49
-21
____
```

7, 14, 21, ____, ____.

7, 14, ____, 28, 35, ____.

7, 14, 21, ____, ____, 42, ____.

Multiples of 7 to 49

Hoops

Name _____
Date _____

P42

 Score 7 points for each hoop.

Draw hoops to make these scores.

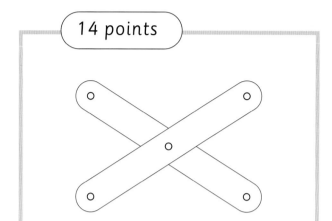

14 points

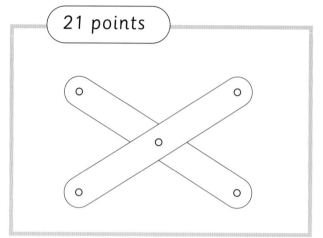

21 points

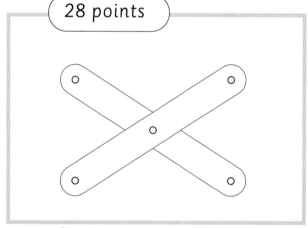

28 points

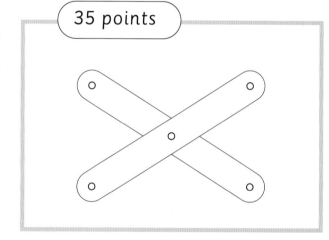

35 points

 7 hoops. How many points?

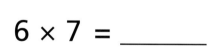

5 × 7 = _____
7 × 5 = _____
35 ÷ 7 = _____
35 ÷ 5 = _____

6 × 7 = _____
7 × 6 = _____
42 ÷ 7 = _____
42 ÷ 6 = _____

Multiples of 7 to 49 ◀ Purple Pupil Book Part 2 pages 50 and 51

What's the difference?

Name _____
Date _____

P43

What's the difference between the amounts in each bag?

Use coins and notes if you want to.

 ✓ or ✗

Subtraction within 500

What's the difference?

Name _____

Date _____

Work with a friend.
Talk about <u>how</u> you work these out.

What's the difference between:

- 85 and 95?
- 99 and 412?
- 500 and 115?
- 136 and 123?
- 99 and 190?
- 341 and 450?
- 299 and 306?
- 400 and 175?

Subtraction within 500

More raffle tickets

Name _____
Date _____

Practise adding!

| 147 | 230 | 147
+ 230
———

| 92 | 132 |

| 209 | 164 |

| 193 | 197 |

| 78 | 184 | 3 | 184
  78
+   3
———

| 63 | 145 | 207 |

```
  142        159         97        114
+  57      + 213      + 232      + 185
—————      —————      —————      —————
             36
```

```
  126        243         59        248
+ 127      + 136      + 241      + 249
—————      —————      —————      —————
```

Addition and subtraction within 500

More raffle tickets

Take away the smaller number from the bigger one.

| 121 | 238 |
| 238 | − 121 |

| 202 |
| 43 |

| 112 |
| 187 |

| 225 |
| 107 |

| 144 |
| 139 |

| 58 |
| 221 |

```
  163        108        249        211
−   4      −  99      − 156      −  60
_____      _____      _____      _____


_____      _____      _____      _____

  178        162        222        250
− 177      −  92      − 111      − 183
_____      _____      _____      _____


_____      _____      _____      _____
```

Addition and subtraction within 500 ◀ Purple Pupil Book Part 2 pages 54 and 55

Multiplying

Name _____
Date _____

P47

Use hundreds, tens and ones. Draw them. Then multiply on paper.

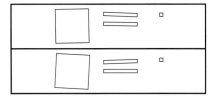
121 times 2

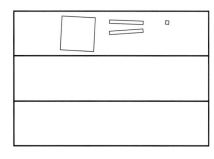
121 times 3

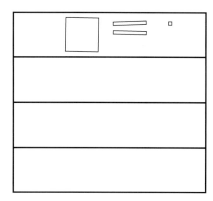
121 times 4

```
  121          121          121
×   2        ×   3        ×   4
_____        _____        _____

_____        _____        _____
```

Use hundreds, tens and ones. **Then** multiply on paper.

```
  161     85      227     108
×   3   ×  5    ×   2   ×   2
_____   ____    _____   _____

_____   ____    _____   _____


  113     65     100
×   4   ×  4   ×   5
_____   ____   _____

_____   ____   _____
```

 ✓ or ✗

Multiplying

Name _____
Date _____

P48

Use hundreds, tens and ones. Draw them.
Then multiply on paper.

144 times 2   155 times 2   166 times 2

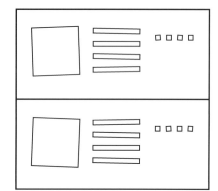 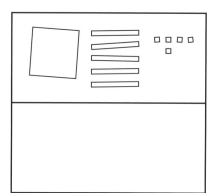 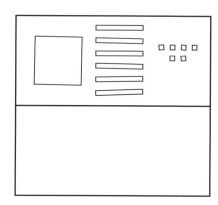

```
   144          155          166
×    2        ×   2        ×   2
_____        _____        _____

_____        _____        _____
```

Multiply on paper. <u>Then</u> use hundreds, tens and ones.

```
   183      63      147      152
×    2    × 3     ×   3    ×   3
_____    ____    _____    _____

_____    ____    _____    _____


   114      48      108
×    4    × 5     ×   4
_____    ____    _____

_____    ____    _____
```

✓ or ✗

Multiplication within 500 ◀ Purple Pupil Book Part 2 pages 56 and 57

Seven times table

Name _____
Date _____

Cut out the eleven tables facts.
Fold along the dotted line and glue flat.

Ask your teacher how to practise with these.

		5 × 7	35
0 × 7	0	6 × 7	42
1 × 7	7	7 × 7	49
2 × 7	14	8 × 7	56
3 × 7	21	9 × 7	63
4 × 7	28	10 × 7	70

Seven times table ◀ Purple Pupil Book Part 2 pages 58 and 59
▶ Copymaster P50

Number Connections © Rose Griffiths 2005
Harcourt Education Ltd

Seven times table

Name _____
Date _____

P50

Fill in the missing numbers.   Check.

7 × 7 = ☐
49 ÷ 7 = ☐

9 × 7 = ☐
63 ÷ 9 = ☐

6 × 7 = ☐
42 ÷ 7 = ☐

7 × 8 = ☐
56 ÷ 7 = ☐

10 × 7 = ☐
☐ × 7 = 63
8 × 7 = ☐
7 × 7 = ☐
☐ × 7 = 42
5 × 7 = ☐
☐ × 7 = 28
☐ × 7 = 21
2 × 7 = ☐
☐ × 7 = 7
0 × 7 = ☐

What is 9 times 7?

What is 8 times 7?

Seven times table ◀ Purple Pupil Book Part 2 pages 58 and 59

Tenths

Name _____
Date _____

How much cake is on each plate?   Write the fractions.

two tenths   five tenths   nine tenths

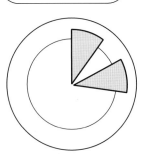 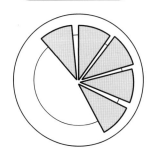 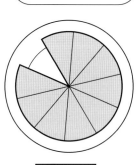

$\frac{2}{10}$

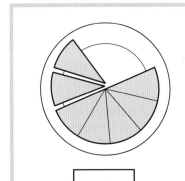 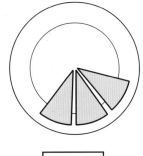 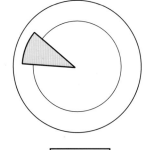

 How much cake is on this tray? $1\frac{4}{10}$

How much on this tray?

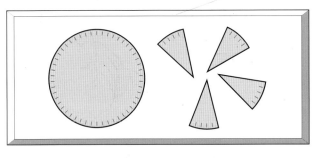 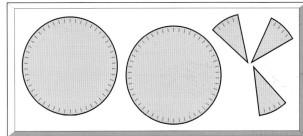

Using halves and tenths

Tenths

Name _____
Date _____

P52

Measure each pencil to the nearest half a centimetre.

7·5 cm

_____

_____

_____

_____

_____

_____

_____

_____

_____

Using halves and tenths ◀ Purple Pupil Book Part 2 pages 60 and 61

Car boot sale

Name _____
Date _____

How much money is this? _____

Divide it by 3.   How much each? _____

How much left over? _____

 Fill in the gaps in our chart.

 Use coins and notes to help you.

Ready reckoner for sharing money between 3 people

How much altogether?	How much each?	How much altogether?	How much each?
£30	£10	£1	33p
£60	£20	£2	
£90		£3	£1
£120		£6	£2
	£50	£9	
£180		£12	
£210		£15	
£240		£18	
£270		£21	
£300		£24	
		£27	

Dividing by 3 within 300

Car boot sale

Name _____
Date _____

P54

You can use your ready reckoner for any amount up to £300.

Ready reckoner for sharing money between 3 people

How much altogether?	How much each?	How much altogether?	How much each?
£30	£10	£1	33p
£60	£20	£2	66p
£90	£30	£3	£1
£120	£40	£6	£2
£150	£50	£9	£3
£180	£60	£12	£4
£210	£70	£15	£5
£240	£80	£18	£6
£270	£90	£21	£7
£300	£100	£24	£8
		£27	£9

In July, we made £83 altogether.

That's £60 + £21 + £2.

So we got £20 + £7 + 66p each. £27.66p each.

Use your ready reckoner for these.

Check with notes and coins.

August
£133 altogether.
How much each?

September
£151 altogether.
How much each?

October
£240 altogether.
How much each?

November
£284 altogether.
How much each?

December
£192 altogether.
How much each?

Dividing by 3 within 300

What's missing?

P55

Name _____
Date _____

Write the missing numbers.

236 − ☐☐☐ = 135

1☐8 + 115 = 243

100 − 72 = ☐8

199 + ☐9 = 288

Check

Now try these.

```
  1 4 8
+   5 ☐
-------
  2 0 2
```

```
  1 3 5
+   1 2 ☐
-------
  2 6 3
```

```
  2 3 2
−   1 1 ☐
-------
  1 1 7
```

```
  1 9 4
×     ☐
-------
  3 8 8
```

```
  1 3 ☐
×     2
-------
  2 7 6
```

```
  ☐ ☐
×   3
-------
  2 4 6
```

Missing numbers and operations ◄ Purple Pupil Book Part 2 pages 64 and 65
► Copymaster P56

Number Connections © Rose Griffiths 2005
Harcourt Education Ltd

What's missing?

6 ☐ 6 = 36   36 ☐ 6 = 6

7 ☐ 5 = 35   6 ☐ 9 = 54

45 ☐ 9 = 5   36 ☐ 9 = 4

374 ☐ 2 = 187

404 ☐ 2 = 202

404 ☐ 2 = 406

404 ☐ 2 = 402

18 ☐ 3 = 54

180 ☐ 79 = 259

250 = 50 ☐ 5

Missing numbers and operations

One hundred bingo

sheet 1 of 2

Print on card if possible. Reusable.

≈One hundred bingo≈

A game for 2, 3 or 4 people.

- **Before you start**
  You need a bingo card and 8 counters each.
  Shuffle the 15 question cards.
  Put them in a pile, face down.

- **How to play**

  Take a question card and read it to everyone.

  If the answer is on their bingo card, they cover it with a counter.

  Now it is your friend's go.

- Keep going until someone says 'Bingo' because they have covered up all their numbers.

◀ Purple Pupil Book Part 2; **Addition and subtraction to 100**

One hundred bingo	One hundred bingo	One hundred bingo	One hundred bingo	One hundred bingo
100 – 3	100 – 12	100 – 17	100 – 25	100 – 36
One hundred bingo	One hundred bingo	One hundred bingo	One hundred bingo	One hundred bingo
100 – 42	100 – 48	100 – 50	100 – 61	100 – 64
One hundred bingo	One hundred bingo	One hundred bingo	One hundred bingo	One hundred bingo
100 – 79	100 – 81	100 – 83	100 – 90	100 – 99

◀ Purple Pupil Book Part 2; use from pages 40 and 41 onwards

One hundred bingo

sheet 2 of 2

Print on card if possible. Reusable.
Cut out the instructions card, 4 bingo cards, and 15 question cards.
Store in a clear zip-top wallet or in an envelope. If possible, include 32 counters.

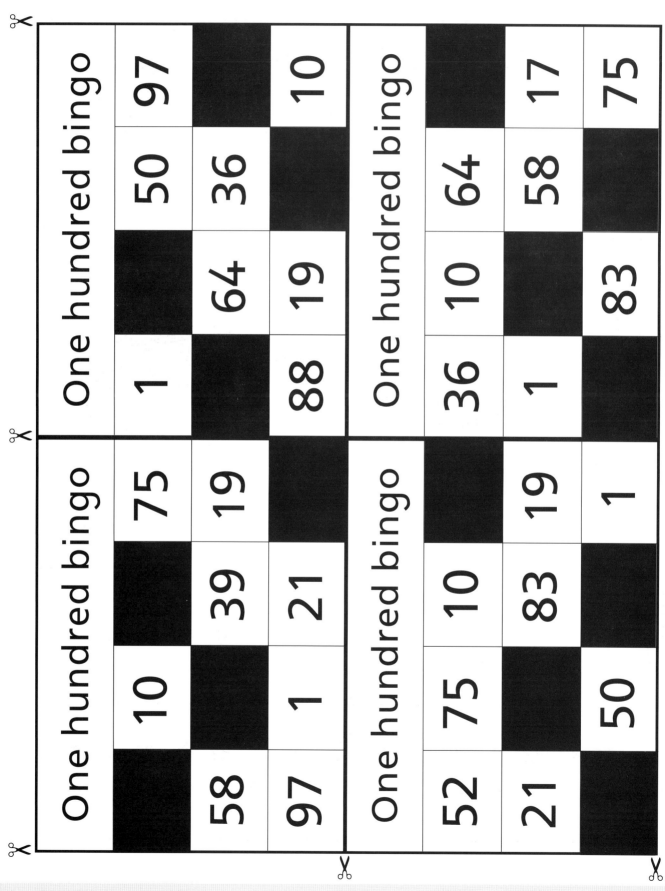

◀ Purple Pupil Book Part 2; use from pages 40 and 41 onwards

Forty-nine game

sheet 1 of 2

Print on card if possible. Reusable.
Cut out the instructions card and 16 star cards. Colour the stars if wished.
Store in a clear zip-top wallet or in an envelope.

≈Forty-nine≈

A game for 1, 2 or 3 people.

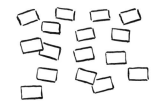

- **Before you start**
  Shuffle the cards.
  Spread them out on the table, face down.

- **How to play**

Turn over 3 cards.
Count the stars.

If you get exactly 49 stars, keep the cards.
If not, turn the cards back over.

Now it is your friend's go.

- Keep going until no one can make any more 49s.

◀ Purple Pupil Book Part 2; **Multiples of 7 to 49**

◀ Purple Pupil Book Part 2; use from pages 50 and 51 onwards

Forty-nine game
sheet 2 of 2

Print on card if possible. Reusable.

▸ Purple Pupil Book Part 2; use from pages 50 and 51 onwards

One thousand

Name _____
Date _____

P61

There are hundreds of people watching us!

How many people in this row?
_____

How many people in this block?
_____

How many people in this block?
_____

How many people watching altogether?
_____

Counting to 1000 ◀ Purple Pupil Book Part 3 pages 68 and 69

Number Connections © Rose Griffiths 2005
Harcourt Education Ltd

Rounding

Name _____
Date _____

P62

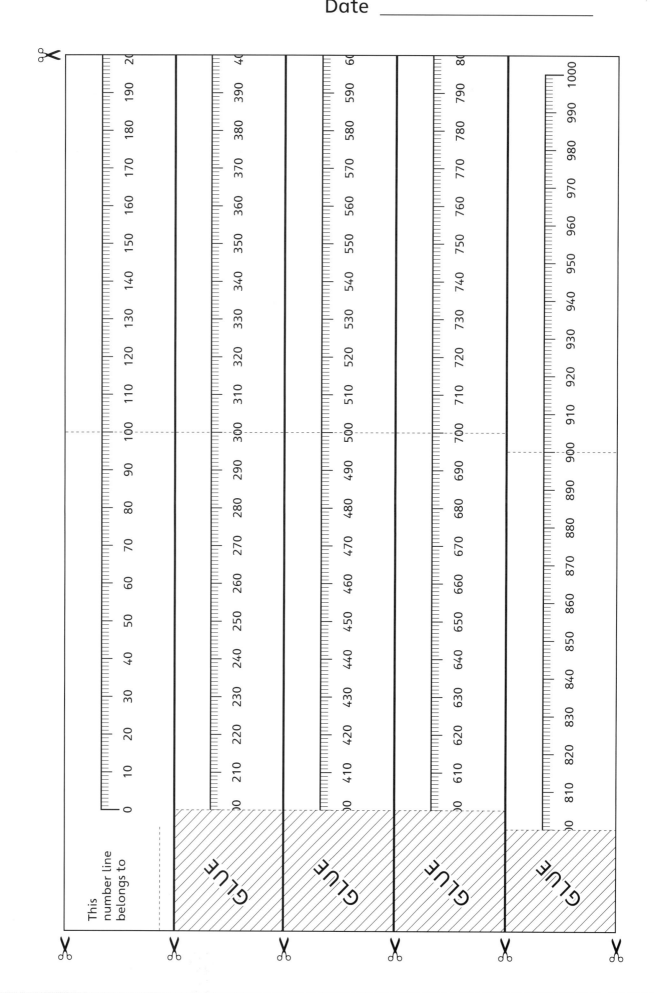

Rounding to the nearest 10 or 100   ◀ Purple Pupil Book Part 3 pages 70 and 71
▶ Copymasters P63 and P64

Rounding

Name _____

Date _____

Make each number with hundreds, tens and ones ... then fill in the chart.

Number	Where is it on the number line?	Rounded to the nearest ten
77	↑ at 77 (between 20 and 100)	80
163	between 90 and 170	
251	between 240 and 320	
419	between 380 and 460	
582	between 510 and 590	
675	between 660 and 740	
896	between 830 and 910	
999	between 920 and 1000	

Rounding to the nearest 10 or 100

Rounding

Name _____
Date _____

Make each number with hundreds, tens and ones ... then fill in the chart.

Number	Where is it on the number line?	Rounded to the nearest hundred
331	300 310 320 **330**↑ 340 350 360 370 380 390 400 410	300
175	90 100 110 120 130 140 150 160 170 180 190 200 210	
392	290 300 310 320 330 340 350 360 370 380 390 400 410	
714	690 700 710 720 730 740 750 760 770 780 790 800 810	
246	190 200 210 220 230 240 250 260 270 280 290 300 310	
483	390 400 410 420 430 440 450 460 470 480 490 500 510	
550	490 500 510 520 530 540 550 560 570 580 590 600 610	
668	590 600 610 620 630 640 650 660 670 680 690 700 710	

Rounding to the nearest 10 or 100 ◂ Purple Pupil Book Part 3 pages 70 and 71

Rough answers

Name _____
Date _____

Five sums are wrong! Can you find them?

Write a <u>rough answer</u> for each sum to help you find the mistakes.

52p + 39p ――― 91p ✓	£1·95 + £7·90 ――― £8·85	£1·35 + £4·20 ――― £5·55
Rough answer: 50p + 40p = 90p	Rough answer:	Rough answer:
£18·10 + £ 3·15 ――― £24·05	£2·99 + £1·98 ――― £4·97	68p + 71p ――― £1·59
Rough answer:	Rough answer:	Rough answer:
£16·40 + £21·95 ――― £38·35	27p + 27p ――― 44p	£ 39·50 + £ 69·95 ――― £101·45
Rough answer:	Rough answer:	Rough answer:

Rounding, using money ◀ Purple Pupil Book Part 3 pages 72 and 73

Hundred squares

Use the hundred squares.

Name _____
Date _____

Fill in the missing numbers.

64 + ☐ = 114

☐ + 30 = 129

215 − 90 = ☐

171 + 80 = ☐

158 + ☐ = 218

86 + ☐ = 286

☐ − 20 = 234

☐ − 200 = 83

165 − 70 = ☐

137 + 80 = ☐

111 + ☐ = 221

Check. ✓ or ✗

1	2	3	4	5	6	7	8	9	10
11	12	13	14	15	16	17	18	19	20
21	22	23	24	25	26	27	28	29	30
31	32	33	34	35	36	37	38	39	40
41	42	43	44	45	46	47	48	49	50
51	52	53	54	55	56	57	58	59	60
61	62	63	64	65	66	67	68	69	70
71	72	73	74	75	76	77	78	79	80
81	82	83	84	85	86	87	88	89	90
91	92	93	94	95	96	97	98	99	100

101	102	103	104	105	106	107	108	109	110
111	112	113	114	115	116	117	118	119	120
121	122	123	124	125	126	127	128	129	130
131	132	133	134	135	136	137	138	139	140
141	142	143	144	145	146	147	148	149	150
151	152	153	154	155	156	157	158	159	160
161	162	163	164	165	166	167	168	169	170
171	172	173	174	175	176	177	178	179	180
181	182	183	184	185	186	187	188	189	190
191	192	193	194	195	196	197	198	199	200

201	202	203	204	205	206	207	208	209	210
211	212	213	214	215	216	217	218	219	220
221	222	223	224	225	226	227	228	229	230
231	232	233	234	235	236	237	238	239	240
241	242	243	244	245	246	247	248	249	250
251	252	253	254	255	256	257	258	259	260
261	262	263	264	265	266	267	268	269	270
271	272	273	274	275	276	277	278	279	280
281	282	283	284	285	286	287	288	289	290
291	292	293	294	295	296	297	298	299	300

Addition and subtraction within 500 ◀ Purple Pupil Book Part 3 pages 74 and 75
▶ Copymaster P67

Hundred squares

Name _____

Date _____

P67

Use the hundred squares.

267 − 32 = _____

298 − 32 = _____

313 − 32 = _____

324 + 43 = _____

357 + 43 = _____

415 + 43 = _____

229 + 101 = _____

323 + 101 = _____

399 + 101 = _____

295 − 50 = _____

425 − 50 = _____

376 − 50 = _____

328 + 33 = _____

249 + 33 = _____

156 + 33 = _____

☐ + 33 = 500

Check. ✓ or ✗

201	202	203	204	205	206	207	208	209	210
211	212	213	214	215	216	217	218	219	220
221	222	223	224	225	226	227	228	229	230
231	232	233	234	235	236	237	238	239	240
241	242	243	244	245	246	247	248	249	250
251	252	253	254	255	256	257	258	259	260
261	262	263	264	265	266	267	268	269	270
271	272	273	274	275	276	277	278	279	280
281	282	283	284	285	286	287	288	289	290
291	292	293	294	295	296	297	298	299	300

301	302	303	304	305	306	307	308	309	310
311	312	313	314	315	316	317	318	319	320
321	322	323	324	325	326	327	328	329	330
331	332	333	334	335	336	337	338	339	340
341	342	343	344	345	346	347	348	349	350
351	352	353	354	355	356	357	358	359	360
361	362	363	364	365	366	367	368	369	370
371	372	373	374	375	376	377	378	379	380
381	382	383	384	385	386	387	388	389	390
391	392	393	394	395	396	397	398	399	400

401	402	403	404	405	406	407	408	409	410
411	412	413	414	415	416	417	418	419	420
421	422	423	424	425	426	427	428	429	430
431	432	433	434	435	436	437	438	439	440
441	442	443	444	445	446	447	448	449	450
451	452	453	454	455	456	457	458	459	460
461	462	463	464	465	466	467	468	469	470
471	472	473	474	475	476	477	478	479	480
481	482	483	484	485	486	487	488	489	490
491	492	493	494	495	496	497	498	499	500

Addition and subtraction within 500   ◀ Purple Pupil Book Part 3 pages 74 and 75

Corner cards

Name _____

Date _____

> Check your spelling with corner cards (Copymaster P89).

4 | 2 | 3

> Shuffle the cards. Use them to make 9 numbers. Write each number ... and its spelling.

Ask your teacher to check your spelling.
Practise any you got wrong.

Place value within 1000
◀ Purple Pupil Book Part 3 pages 76 and 77
▶ Copymaster P69

Corner cards

Name _____

Date _____

P69

Use corner cards (Copymaster P89) to make up sums.

Don't use 900 800 700 600 or 500

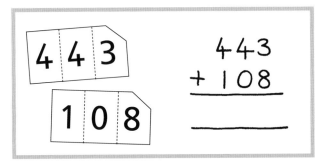

443
+108
____

Do the sums yourself ... or give them to a friend!

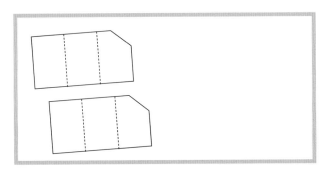   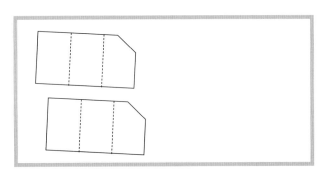

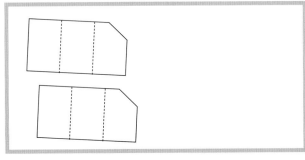   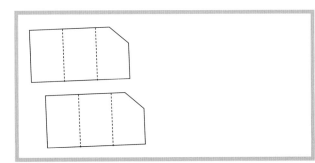

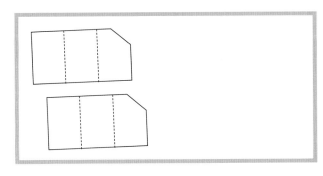   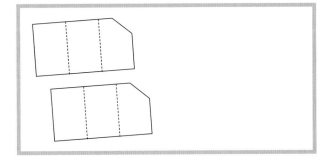

Check. ✓ or ✗

Place value within 1000

Boxes and bones

Name _____
Date _____

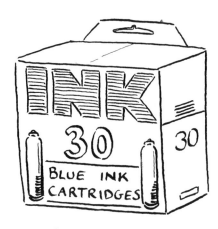

30 ink cartridges in a box
How many in:

2 boxes? _____

4 boxes? _____

5 boxes? _____

8 boxes? _____

10 boxes? _____

Fill in the missing numbers:

| 0 | 30 | 60 | | 120 | | 180 | | 240 |

| 300 | 270 | | | 180 | 150 | 120 | | |

90 + 30 = _____

90 + 60 = _____

90 + 90 = _____

90 + 120 = _____

90 + 150 = _____

90 + 180 = _____

 30
× 3
———

 30
× 4
———

 30
× 6
———

 30
× 7
———

 30
× 8
———

 30
× 9
———

Arithmetic within 750

Boxes and bones

Name _____
Date _____

APPROX. is short for APPROXIMATE.
What does it mean?

_____

_____

How many drawing pins in:

2 boxes? _____   3 boxes? _____   4 boxes? _____

I need 4 drawing pins to put up a picture.

How many drawing pins for:

3 pictures? _____   7 pictures? _____   8 pictures? _____

10 pictures? _____   11 pictures? _____   12 pictures? _____

How many pictures could I put up with 60 drawing pins? _____

4) 80   4) 100   4) 700

Arithmetic within 750

Stamps

Name _____

Date _____

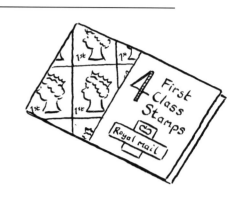

The machine sells books of 4 stamps.

How many stamps in:

6 books? _____   10 books? _____   16 books? _____

How many stamps in:

20 books? _____   3 books? _____   23 books? _____

How many stamps in:

11 books? _____   8 books? _____   19 books? _____

I need 16 stamps. How many books of 4?

_____

I need 10 stamps. How many books of 4?

_____

```
   35        17        22        50        92
 ×  4      ×  4      ×  4      ×  4      ×  4
 ____      ____      ____      ____      ____

 ____      ____      ____      ____      ____
```

4) 60   4) 92   4) 68

Arithmetic within 750

Stamps

Name _____
Date _____

P73

Put stamps on each parcel.
Don't stick them on until you've tried all four!

"This needs £3·40."

Mo Smith,
24 Forest Road,
Blaby.

"£1·60"

Jenny Roberts,
39 Bagg Lane,
Wanstead.

"92p"

K. Parkar,
147 Leicester Road,
London,
N12 8PQ.

"£1·45"

Mr. & Mrs. Price,
56 Meadow Street,
Leeds.

FRAGILE

"Did you have any stamps left over?"

_____

✂ -

£1 £1 £1   50p   10p   £2   2p

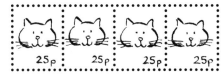 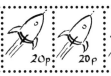

25p 25p 25p 25p   20p 20p 20p 20p 20p

Arithmetic within 750 ◀ Purple Pupil Book Part 3 pages 80 and 81

More corner cards

Name _____
Date _____

P74

Add these.

| 297 | 697 |
| 612 | 212 |

| 43 | 543 |
| 580 | 80 |

| 102 | 109 |
| 409 | 402 |

| 345 | 389 |
| 289 | 245 |

Check. ✓ or ✗

Addition within 1000 ◀ Purple Pupil Book Part 3 pages 82 and 83
▶ Copymaster P75

More corner cards

Name _____

Date _____

P75

Use corner cards to make up sums.

Don't use 9 0 0   8 0 0   7 0 0   6 0 0 or 5 0 0

Do the sums yourself ... or give them to a friend.

400+100+40+2=

Write each number.   Write what you do.

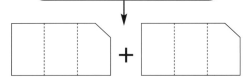

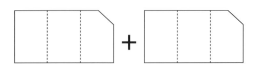

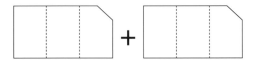

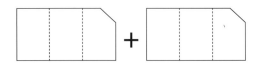

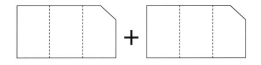

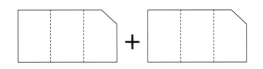

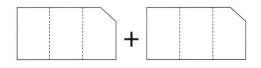

Addition within 1000 ◄ Purple Pupil Book Part 3 pages 82 and 83

Eight times table

Name _____
Date _____

Cut out the eleven tables facts.
Fold along the dotted line and glue flat.

Ask your teacher how to practise with these.

5×8	40
0×8 0	6×8 48
1×8 8	7×8 56
2×8 16	8×8 64
3×8 24	9×8 72
4×8 32	10×8 80

Eight times table ◀ Purple Pupil Book Part 3 pages 84 and 85
▶ Copymaster P77

Eight times table

Name _____
Date _____

Fill in the missing numbers.
Check with a calculator.

8 × 8 = ☐
64 ÷ 8 = ☐

7 × 8 = ☐
56 ÷ 8 = ☐

6 × 8 = ☐
48 ÷ 8 = ☐

9 × 8 = ☐
72 ÷ 8 = ☐

10 × 8 = ☐
☐ × 8 = 72
8 × 8 = ☐
☐ × 8 = 56
☐ × 8 = 48
5 × 8 = ☐
☐ × 8 = 32
3 × 8 = ☐
2 × 8 = ☐
☐ × 8 = 8
0 × 8 = ☐

What is 7 times 8?

What is 8 times 8?

Add or take away

Name _____
Date _____

Find these adding and taking away words.

+	−
add	take away
plus	minus
increase	decrease
more	less
total	subtract

B	A	D	D	C	M	O	R	E
T	A	K	E	A	W	A	Y	Z
D	E	H	C	G	I	L	J	S
I	N	C	R	E	A	S	E	U
M	N	F	E	K	O	L	P	B
R	S	U	A	Q	T	E	V	T
P	L	U	S	T	O	S	X	R
Y	A	C	E	E	T	S	F	A
Z	D	W	B	H	A	I	J	C
M	I	N	U	S	L	G	K	T

Fill in $+$ or $-$.

128 ☐ 19 = 147   500 ☐ 136 = 364

128 ☐ 19 = 109   500 ☐ 136 = 636

```
  263         76        199        462
+ 148      + 451      + 299      + 485
-----      -----      -----      -----


  390        528        660        750
− 154      − 250      − 142      − 209
-----      -----      -----      -----
```

Addition and subtraction within 750

Add or take away

Name _____
Date _____

Write each sum and work it out.

Seven hundred and fifty take away ninety-three

```
 750
- 93
____
```

Four hundred and sixty-five plus one hundred and thirty-nine

Five hundred and seventy minus two hundred and one

One hundred and twenty-four subtract eighty-three

Twenty-eight add three hundred and forty-seven

The difference between six hundred, and four hundred

Two hundred and fifty-eight add one hundred and forty-two

Six hundred and seventy-two take away one hundred and thirteen

Addition and subtraction within 750

Speedy tables K

1 2 3 minute test

Name _____

Date _____

6 × 4 = ____   100 ÷ 10 = ____   9 × 9 = ____

8 × 0 = ____   56 ÷ 7 = ____   25 ÷ 5 = ____

7 × 6 = ____   48 ÷ 8 = ____   4 × 8 = ____

3 × 9 = ____   21 ÷ 3 = ____   64 ÷ 8 = ____

6 × 6 = ____   45 ÷ 9 = ____   5 × 6 = ____

9 × 8 = ____   70 ÷ 7 = ____   16 ÷ 4 = ____

2 × 8 = ____   28 ÷ 4 = ____   Score: ____

Mental recall of tables facts ◀ Purple Pupil Book Part 3 pages 88 and 89 onwards

---

Speedy tables L

1 2 3 minute test

Name _____

Date _____

3 × 6 = ____   24 ÷ 4 = ____   8 × 8 = ____

6 × 7 = ____   80 ÷ 10 = ____   100 ÷ 10 = ____

5 × 8 = ____   49 ÷ 7 = ____   7 × 9 = ____

9 × 6 = ____   81 ÷ 9 = ____   2 ÷ 2 = ____

0 × 4 = ____   56 ÷ 8 = ____   4 × 9 = ____

8 × 9 = ____   21 ÷ 7 = ____   36 ÷ 6 = ____

6 × 8 = ____   24 ÷ 3 = ____   Score: ____

Mental recall of tables facts ◀ Purple Pupil Book Part 3 pages 88 and 89 onwards

More multiplying

Name _____
Date _____

P81

Draw hundreds, tens and ones. Then multiply on paper.

135 times 3   135 times 4   135 times 5

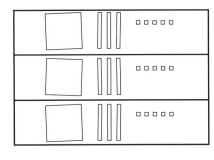
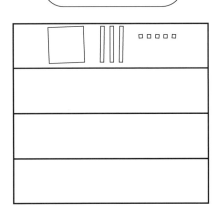

```
  135        135        135
×   3      ×   4      ×   5
_____      _____      _____

_____      _____      _____
```

Use hundreds, tens and ones. Then multiply on paper.

```
  170        150        199        156
×   4      ×   5      ×   3      ×   4
_____      _____      _____      _____

_____      _____      _____      _____


  184        207         98
×   4      ×   3      ×   5
_____      _____      _____
```

 ✓ or ✗

```
_____      _____      _____
```

Multiplication within 750

More multiplying

Name _____
Date _____

P82

| 1 0 0 | × 6 = _____ |
| 3 | × 6 = _____ |
so | 1 0 3 | × 6 = _____

$$\begin{array}{r} 103 \\ \times6 \\ \hline \\ \hline \end{array}$$

1 0 0	× 5 = _____
4 0	× 5 = _____
7	× 5 = _____
so | 1 4 7 | × 5 = _____

$$\begin{array}{r} 147 \\ \times5 \\ \hline \\ \hline \end{array}$$

| 9 0 | × 6 = _____ |
| 4 | × 6 = _____ |
so | 9 4 | × 6 = _____

$$\begin{array}{r} 94 \\ \times6 \\ \hline \\ \hline \end{array}$$

| 1 0 0 | × 4 = _____ |
| 8 0 | × 4 = _____ |
so | 1 8 0 | × 4 = _____

$$\begin{array}{r} 180 \\ \times4 \\ \hline \\ \hline \end{array}$$

| 8 0 | × 5 = _____ |
| 9 | × 5 = _____ |
so | 8 9 | × 5 = _____

$$\begin{array}{r} 89 \\ \times5 \\ \hline \\ \hline \end{array}$$

Multiplication within 750 ◀ Purple Pupil Book Part 3 pages 90 and 91

Halves

Name _____
Date _____

I'll meet you half-way!

Measure the line: __11__ cm.
Halve the length: __6·5__ cm.

Measure the line and put a cross half-way along.

Measure the line: _____ cm.
Halve the length: _____ cm.

Measure and put a cross half-way along.

Measure the line: _____ cm.   Measure the line: _____ cm.
Halve it: _____ cm.   Halve it: _____ cm.
Put a cross half-way.   Put a cross half-way.

Measure the line: _____ cm.
Halve it: _____ cm.
Put a cross half-way.

Holidays

Name _____
Date _____

Use notes and coins to help you.

Check

Chalet in Scotland

£590
(maximum 5 people)

How much per person ...
- if 2 people go? _____
- if 3 people go? _____
- if 4 people go? _____
- if 5 people go? _____

Villa on the Costa del Sol

£720
(maximum 6 people)

How much per person ...
- if 2 people go? _____
- if 3 people go? _____
- if 4 people go? _____
- if 5 people go? _____

Caravan in Hunstanton

£380
(maximum 6 people)

How much per person ...
- if 2 people go? _____
- if 3 people go? _____
- if 4 people go? _____
- if 5 people go? _____

Holidays

Name _____

Date _____

P85

Work with a partner.

Make up some holiday questions for each other.

Fantastic caravan in ....

£ ......

(maximum 5 people)

How much per person ...
- if ☐ people go? _____
- if ☐ people go? _____

Chalet in ....

£ ......

(maximum 6 people)

How much per person ...
- if ☐ people go? _____
- if ☐ people go? _____

Villa in ....

£ ......

(maximum 5 people)

How much per person ...
- if ☐ people go? _____
- if ☐ people go? _____

Dividing by 2, 3, 4 or 5 within 750 ◀ Purple Pupil Book Part 3 pages 94 and 95

Number Connections © Rose Griffiths 2005
Harcourt Education Ltd

Rough total game

sheet 1 of 2

Print on card if possible. Reusable.
Cut out the instructions card and 24 playing cards.
Store in a clear zip-top wallet or in an envelope.

≈Rough total≈

A game for 2 or 3 people.

- **Before you start**
  Shuffle the cards.
  Spread them out on the table, face down.

- **How to play**

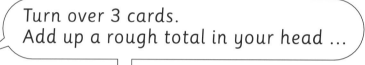

Turn over 3 cards.
Add up a rough total in your head ...

while your friend adds them exactly, on the calculator.

10p + 30p + 40p ...

rough total is 80p.

10p + 27p + 39p ...

exact total is 76p.

- If your rough total is reasonable, keep the cards.
  If not, put them back.

- **Now it is your friend's go.**

◀ Purple Pupil Book Part 3; **Rounding, using money**

Number Connections © Rose Griffiths 2005
Harcourt Education Ltd

◀ Purple Pupil Book Part 3; use from pages 72 and 73 onwards

Rough total game
sheet 2 of 2

Print 2 copies, on card if possible. Reusable.
Colour if wished. Cut into 24 cards.

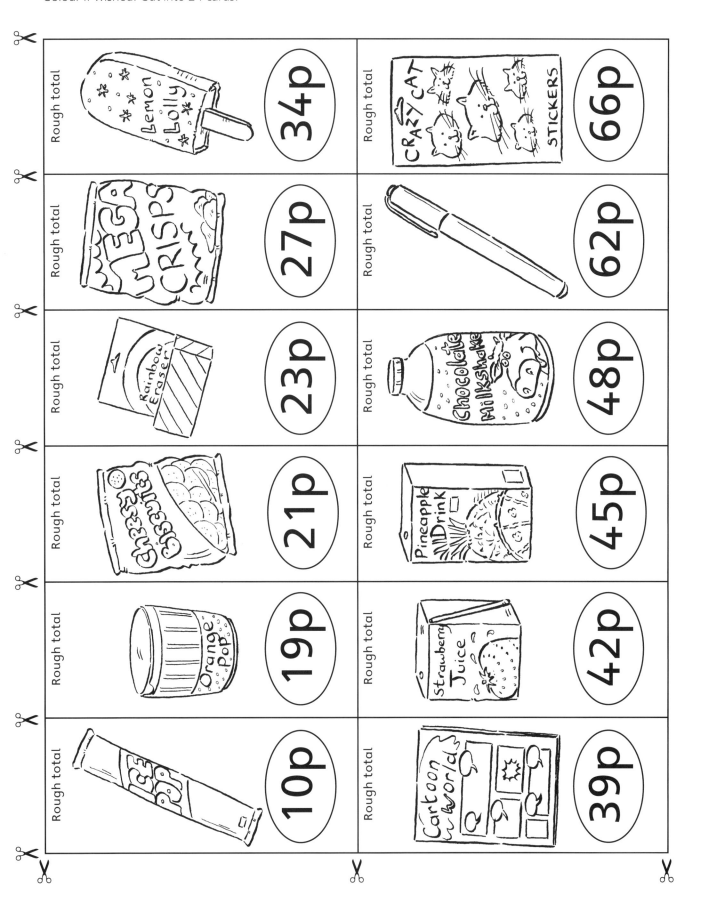

◀ Purple Pupil Book Part 3; use from pages 72 and 73 onwards

999 game

sheet 1 of 2

Print on card if possible. Reusable.
Cut out the instructions card and 27 corner cards.
Store in a clear zip-top wallet or in an envelope.

≈999≈

A game for 2 people.

- **Before you start**
  Spread the corner cards on the table, face up.

- **How to play**

Choose a hundreds, a tens and a ones card to make a number.

Ask your friend to make the number which will add to yours, to make 999.

- **Check with a calculator.**

$7\;4\;8 + 2\;5\;1 = 999$ ✓

- **Have 9 turns each … or more!**

◀ Purple Pupil Book Part 3; **Place value within 1000**

Number Connections © Rose Griffiths 2005
Harcourt Education Ltd

999 game
sheet 2 of 2

Print on card if possible. Reusable.
Cut into 27 corner cards, with one corner cut off each.

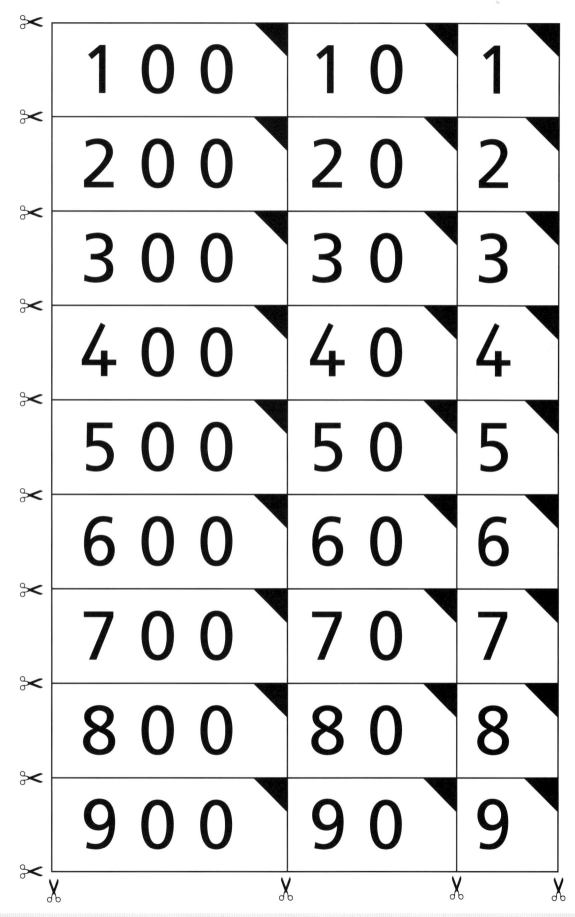

◀ Purple Pupil Book Part 3; use from pages 76 and 77 onwards

Eights game

sheet 1 of 3

Print on card if possible. Reusable.
Cut out the instructions card and 9 stamp cards. Colour the stamps if wished. Store in a clear zip-top wallet or in an envelope.

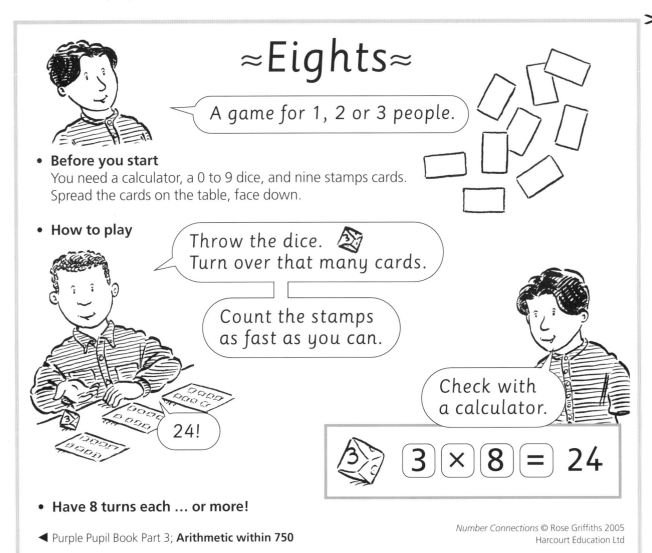

≈Eights≈

A game for 1, 2 or 3 people.

- **Before you start**
  You need a calculator, a 0 to 9 dice, and nine stamps cards. Spread the cards on the table, face down.

- **How to play**
  Throw the dice. Turn over that many cards.
  Count the stamps as fast as you can.
  Check with a calculator.

  $3 \times 8 = 24$

- **Have 8 turns each … or more!**

◀ Purple Pupil Book Part 3; **Arithmetic within 750**

If you wish, make your own stamps cards, using real stamps.

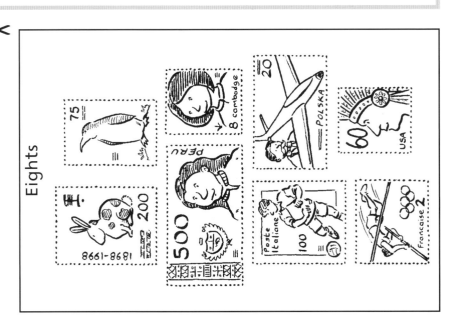

Eights game
sheet 2 of 3

Print on card if possible. Reusable.

Purple Pupil Book Part 3; use from pages 80 and 81 onwards

Eights game
sheet 3 of 3

Print on card if possible. Reusable.

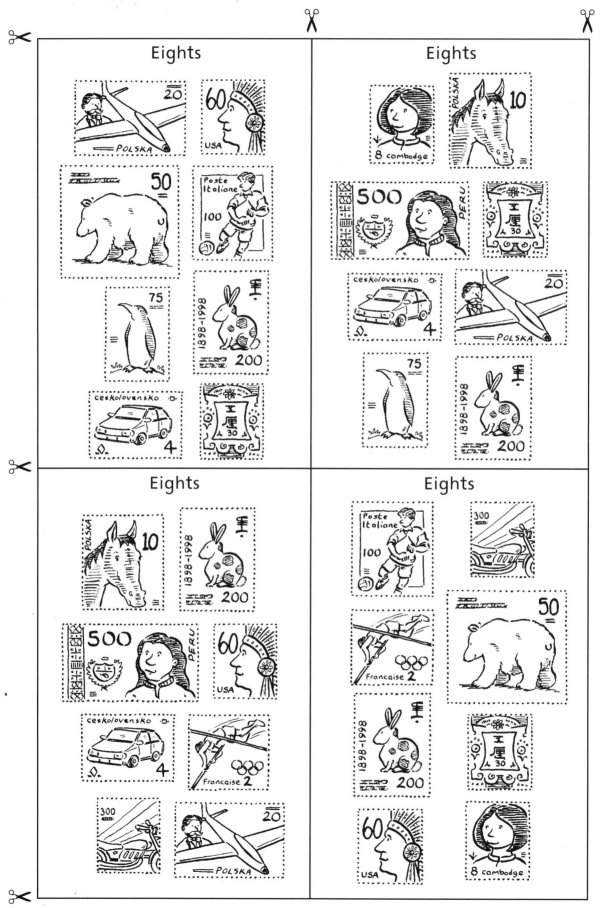

◀ Purple Pupil Book Part 3; use from pages 80 and 81 onwards